Jes___

My Good Shepherd

Mark 6:34, John 10:11–18 for children
Written by Erik Rottmann
Illustrated by Yoshi Miyake

Arch® Books
Copyright © 2005 Concordia Publishing House
3558 S. Jefferson Avenue, St. Louis, MO 63118-3968
1-800-325-3040 www.cph.org

Whenever Jesus went to preach
His Gospel to the poor,
He saw that those who came to hear
Were often sad or sore.

They looked like weak and feeble lambs
Without a shepherd dear;
Harassed and helpless little sheep
With danger drawing near.

So their Good Shepherd, Jesus Christ,
With mercy and with love,
Began to teach about God's grace,
Sent to them from above.

His Words gave comfort in distress;
His Words gave peace of mind.
His Words brought hearing to the deaf
And gave sight to the blind.

A faithful shepherd watches close.
He gently guards each lamb.
He never leaves his flock alone.
He guides them with his hand.

But sometimes sheep will run away.
They leave their shepherd's arm.
Then danger quickly rises up
And threatens them with harm.

So their good shepherd follows them
And makes them safe and sound.
He swings his staff and chases back
The dangers all around.

Just as a shepherd guards his flock
From lion, wolf or bear,
Jesus promised to protect
Each person in His care.

The Bible says that we, like sheep,
Have each one gone astray.
Through sin we walked away from God
And followed our own way.

So God put onto our dear Lord
Our sin and fault and blame.
Then Jesus carried to the cross
Each person's guilt and shame.

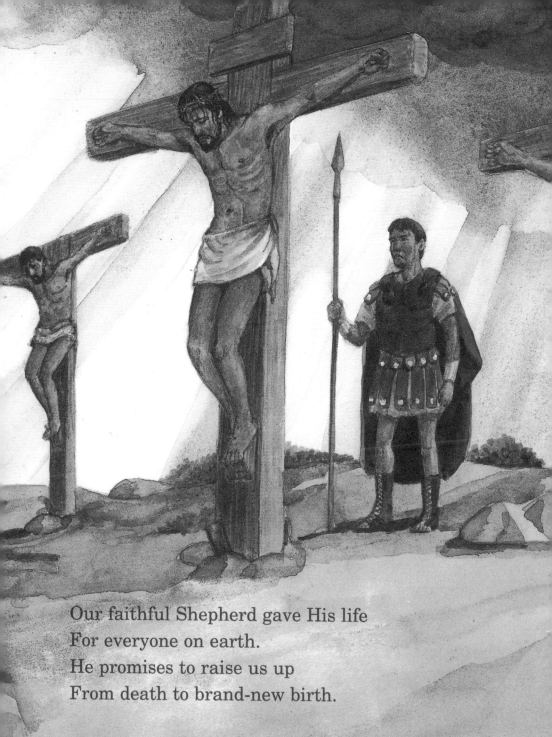

Our faithful Shepherd gave His life
For everyone on earth.
He promises to raise us up
From death to brand-new birth.

He washes in baptismal rain
Your every flaw and sin.
He opens up your heart to faith
And sends His Spirit in.

He comforts you in each distress,
In every care and fear.
He teaches you eternal life
And through His Word draws near.

His Words make you His tender lamb.
His Words will guard your day.
His Words will build you up in faith
So you can always pray:

"My Shepherd is Lord Jesus Christ,
My good and gentle King,
Who guards and keeps me in His care
No matter what life brings.

"Never will He let me go;
He'll not leave me alone.
He'll bring me safely through all things
To His eternal home."

Dear Parents,

"When Jesus landed and saw a large crowd, He had compassion on them, because they were like sheep without a shepherd. So He began teaching them many things" (Mark 6:34). With these words, St. Mark shows us the way in which our Lord Jesus loves and cares for His people: He *teaches* them.

A faithful shepherd devotes his life to his flock, sacrificing his comfort and safety for the sake of the sheep in his care. In the same way, Jesus our Good Shepherd sacrificed Himself for us that we might be preserved from every enemy that would scatter and destroy us.

Use this story of the Good Shepherd to teach your children about God's love for them—and for you—in Christ. Discuss with them the sorts of things that make them feel threatened or afraid. Then tell them how Jesus uses His powerful and life-giving words to preserve and protect His dear sheep from all harm. He *teaches* those who are harassed and helpless, like sheep without a shepherd. He does not merely speak words for you to learn, but He gives you eternal Words that create faith, increase trust, and deliver eternal life.

The Author